Little Learning Labs

GEOLOGY
for Kids

Brimming with creative inspiration, how-to projects, and useful information to enrich your everyday life, Quarto Knows is a favorite destination for those pursuing their interests and passions. Visit our site and dig deeper with our books into your area of interest: Quarto Creates, Quarto Cooks, Quarto Homes, Quarto Lives, Quarto Drives, Quarto Explores, Quarto Gifts, or Quarto Kids.

First Published in 2019 by Quarry Books, an imprint of The Quarto Group,
100 Cummings Center, Suite 265-D, Beverly, MA 01915, USA.
T (978) 282-9590 F (978) 283-2742 QuartoKnows.com

Quarry Books titles are also available at discount for retail, wholesale, promotional, and bulk purchase. For details, contact the Special Sales Manager by email at specialsales@quarto.com or by mail at The Quarto Group, Attn: Special Sales Manager, 100 Cummings Center, Suite 265-D, Beverly, MA 01915, USA.

10 9 8 7 6 5 4 3 2 1

ISBN: 978-1-63159-811-1

Digital edition published in 2019

The content for this book previously appeared in the book *Geology Lab for Kids*, by Garrett Romaine (Quarry Books, 2017).

Library of Congress Cataloging-in-Publication Data available under *Geology Lab for Kids*.

Book Design: Kathie Alexander
Cover Image: Patrick Smith Photography
Photography: Patrick Smith Photography, except images by Shutterstock
on pages 4, 6, 12, 22, 30, 36, 48, 58, 66 (top), 68, 72, 74 (top).

Printed in China

Borax, also known by its chemical name sodium tetraborate, is a trademarked product in the United States from the Rio Tinto Group. In this book, Borax is used as a material in lab 3.

Little Learning Labs

GEOLOGY
for Kids

Activities for STEAM Learners

26 Projects to Explore Rocks, Gems, Geodes, Crystals, Fossils, and Other Wonders of the Earth's Surface

Garret Romaine

QUARRY

CONTENTS

INTRODUCTION

Geology is the science of the Earth and learning to describe what you see so that someone else can understand. Once you get good at talking about the world around you, it's not hard to take that to the next level and figure out what happened to the Earth in the past, even if you can't see it happening today. Nobody has ever traveled to the middle of the Earth, but by making models based on places we have been, we think we know what's going on there. That's science—make a prediction, see if you can prove it, and then apply it to bigger questions.

In this book, you will learn a lot about the way things happen and why. You'll be introduced to the science behind processes you see all around you, and you'll learn to think about the Earth in new and exciting ways. Some of the most important parts of geology come down to very simple concepts—gravity, friction, heat, and water. Some things you'll learn about are:

How to make your own crystals. Learn how crystals form and how to tell them apart. All rocks contain crystals, so this is a perfect place to begin.

The differences between major rock types. Learn how the three main groups of rocks form. You'll discover the forces behind igneous, sedimentary, and metamorphic rocks.

Identification and prospecting. See how scientists tell gems from ordinary crystals and how they learn to look for valuable rocks. Once you learn how to tell one mineral from another, you can start to identify the rocks you find all around you.

How things break down (entropy). See how Earth's forces take fresh, young lava flows and turn them into sand at the beach. The sun plays a part, too, and so do plants. Entropy is the idea that everything breaks down eventually. Steel will rust, and mountains will crumble.

Fossils are the clues of life. Our planet has an amazing fossil record to discover. Learn how scientists uncover clues about what Earth was like millions of years ago.

Why space rocks are important. Learn how comets and meteorites can rearrange the Earth's surface.

Rocks can be more than just rocks. Now that you know what's going on inside a rock or crystal, you'll see what you can do with rocks and minerals in work and play. There are lots of ways to display your treasures and use them to create art or everyday objects. Early humans used the materials around them for tools and you can, too.

Geology uses a set of vocabulary words. Many of the words are ancient, dating back to the earliest times. Many foreign languages have found their way into geology as well. For example, the German words *schist* (pronounced "shist") and *gneiss* (pronounced "nice") both describe certain metamorphic rocks. Two Hawaiian words— *aa* (pronounced "ah-ah") and *pahoehoe* (pronounced "pa-hoy-hoy")—are used to describe lava flows, as there is so much volcanic activity on the Hawaiian islands. Aa lava is jagged and blocky, while pahoehoe lava is ropy and runny. These are just some of many examples.

Geology is based on observations and predictions that are part of the scientific model. Fortunately, the Earth works in a way we can understand, so if we can make the right model, we can use what we see in that model to predict other forces. We can measure things at a small scale, and we can make models to teach others. Even simple, fun projects can show the larger world at work. The labs and projects in this book will help you understand how much fun it is to learn about the world around you.

The best part is that most of these labs don't require a lot of expensive materials; many of them are easy to complete with items you find in your parents' kitchen or garage. But if you want to get super serious about understanding the world around you, this book will help you with that, too. Some of the materials will take a little more searching to find, and you may want to get help ordering items online that you can't easily track down. That can be part of the fun, too—you may get to go to thrift stores or second-hand stores to find used pots and pans, for example. You should also expect to visit a craft store to find some of the items you'll need.

And finally, be sure to visit a local rock and gem shop to find samples, books, tools, and advice on how to begin your own collection.

Over the years, I have spent countless hours working with kids just like you in lectures, at demonstrations, and even as a merit badge counselor, helping them understand the world around them. Many of the labs here are time-tested, having been around for years. But some are completely new or bring a new twist to an old idea. We'll start with simple concepts and then connect the dots to bigger ideas. In that way, these labs are like building blocks: start small and keep building. At some point, you'll probably find that you are learning how more and more pieces of the puzzle fit together. That's always been the most enjoyable for me, showing others how all the different things they already know can apply. It's always a lot of fun to go to the beach and pick up a few rocks, but when you know how to identify the rocks and explain how they got there, you feel like a detective solving a big riddle. Some of you may even go on to careers in the Earth sciences or become planetary scientists who travel to distant locales. I hope that's the case!

Let's get started. And remember: No one likes a messy lab partner!

IDENTIFYING ROCKS AND MINERALS

Rocks and minerals are the building blocks of the Earth. Minerals have a chemical formula, with an exact number of atoms of different elements. For example, calcite is $CaCO_3$—it has one calcium atom, one carbon atom, and three oxygen atoms. Minerals can be identified with tests for streak, hardness, crystal angle, and density, which you will learn in these labs. Rocks are made up of different minerals, in lots of combinations, and they can be glued, pressed, or melted together in many ways. To identify rocks, you need to know what minerals are in them, how they are held together, and how they formed. You will also learn about the three "families" of rocks: sedimentary, igneous, and metamorphic.

Shown here are many of the most common minerals that you can find, plus a few that are rare and valuable. Most of the rocks listed here are very common. If you can learn to identify them, you can start to explain the world around you.

Minerals

Calcite

Epidote

Feldspar

Fluorite

Garnet

Gold

Gypsum

Jade

Malachite

Muscovite mica

Pyrite

Quartz

Rocks

Agate

Basalt

Chalcedony

Chert

Conglomerate

Gneiss

Granite

Jasper

Limestone

Marble

Meteorite

Mudstone

Obsidian

Opal

Petrified wood

Quartzite

Rhyolite

Sandstone

Schist

CRYSTALS, CLUSTERS, AND GEODES

Maybe you've heard this joke: "How do you eat an elephant?" The answer is "one bite at a time." So, how do you "build" the Earth? That's simple, too: one atom at a time.

Atoms are the basic building blocks of crystals, and since all rocks are made up of crystals, the more you know about atoms, the better.

Crystals come in a variety of shapes that scientists call *habits*. Common crystal habits include squares, triangles, and six-sided hexagons. Usually crystals form when liquids cool, such as when you create ice cubes. Many times, crystals form in ways that do not allow for perfect shapes. If conditions are too cold, too hot, or there isn't enough source material, they can form strange, twisted shapes.

But when conditions are right, we see beautiful displays. Usually, this involves a slow, steady environment where the individual atoms have plenty of time to join and fit perfectly into what's known as the *crystal lattice*. This is the basic structure of atoms that is seen time after time. In nature, crystals usually form together in clusters because there is more than enough material. They are a lot easier to enjoy, because you won't need a magnifying glass to see them, like you would with some individual crystals.

Crystals generally start as a liquid, and then cool down slowly enough to form proper "faces" on their crystal structure. A term you should know is *vug*—a pocket or gap in a vein where bigger crystals can form. Many of the most valuable gems grow in vugs, where conditions are often perfect to slowly form larger, better crystals. In this Unit, we will build our own individual crystals, watch them grow in groups, and make a geode.

TASTY TREATS

Build a solid sugar crystal, sometimes called rock candy.

MATERIALS

- 1 cup (236 ml) of water
- Pan for boiling water
- 3+ cups (600+ g) of white sugar
- Metal stirring spoon
- 3–4 drops of food coloring of any color
- 12" (30 cm) of rough yarn or twine
- Scissors
- 6" (15 cm) pencil
- ½-quart (473 ml) narrow-mouth glass Mason jar
- Round, hard ring-shaped candy (or other clean weight)
- Paper towel, napkin, or washcloth

Safety Tips

- Be cautious around the stove to avoid burns.
- Ask an adult for help boiling the water.

PROTOCOL

STEP 1: Add the water to the pan and boil the water on the stove. A microwave is not recommended.

STEP 2: Stir in the sugar slowly, adding as much as possible until it starts to build up at the bottom. Don't stop: you want your solution to be saturated.

STEP 3: Add a few drops of food coloring to make a rich color. Let cool.

STEP 4: Cut a piece of yarn or twine that is 1 inch (2.5 cm) longer than the height of your jar.

STEP 5: Tie one end of the twine or yarn around the pencil, leaving enough string to dangle the length of your jar without touching the bottom. Tie the other end around the piece of candy.

STEP 6: Moisten the string thoroughly with water, and then sprinkle lightly with sugar so that you create small "seed" crystals. Let dry for ten minutes.

STEP 7: Pour the cooled water mixture into the jar. The solution needs to be cooled so that it won't dissolve your seed crystal. Avoid pouring any of the little sugar crystals from the bottom of the pan.

STEP 8: Place the pencil across the mouth of the jar so the candy floats in the mixture.

STEP 9: Place a paper towel, napkin, or washcloth over the jar and set it aside in a corner of the kitchen. Do not disturb.

STEP 10: Check on the string after a day; it should already host small, square sugar crystals.

STEP 11: Leave the string in the solution for at least a week. You can add more solution if you want to grow bigger crystals.

 Creative Enrichment

1. What happens if you use fishing line or very smooth string?

2. Use a magnifying glass or hand lens to look at the hardened crystals. What shape are they? Would you call that a square or a cube?

3. What would happen if there were twice as much water— would the sugar ever crystallize on the string?

THE SCIENCE BEHIND THE FUN

Growing sugar crystals is a great way to learn how saturated solutions are unstable at room temperature. The solution cannot handle any more sugar when the temperature falls, and crystals start to form. Over time, some water will evaporate, while solid sugar begins to crystallize. That's why it's important to avoid using a lid.

Sugar is a crystal with the formula $C_{12}H_{22}O_{11}$. That's a lot of atoms: twelve carbon atoms, twenty-two hydrogen atoms, and eleven oxygen atoms. They form as cubes, and their crystal "habit" is known as *cubic*. If you measure the angles with a protractor, each elbow should be 90 degrees.

If you keep adding sugar solution to the jar, you can grow enormous crystals. This is a key to understanding how crystals form in the Earth. A solution that keeps flowing through cracks in the rocks will refresh the small crystals and they will keep growing. If you find small crystals in a rock, they probably didn't get a lot of time to grow. But large crystals usually tell mineralogists that growth conditions were perfect for a long time.

SALTY SQUARES

Grow your own perfect cube of salty perfection.

MATERIALS

- 1 cup (235 ml) of water
- 7–8 tablespoons (126–144 g) of table salt (sodium chloride, NaCl). Iodized is okay.
- Food coloring (optional)
- Piece of cardboard (optional)
- Clean, clear container
- Saucer (optional)
- 12" (30 cm) string or fishing line (optional)
- Scissors (optional)
- Pencil or butter knife (optional)
- Paper towel or coffee filter (optional)

 Safety Tips

- Don't get salt in your eyes.
- Wash hands quickly after handling salt.
- Ask an adult for help boiling the water.
- Be cautious around the cooking stove to avoid burns.

Creative Enrichment

1. Experiment with different types of table salt and water. See if there is any difference in the appearance of the crystals.

2. If you are trying for the "perfect crystal" use un-iodized salt and distilled water. Impurities in either the salt or water can aid in *dislocation*, in which new crystals don't stack perfectly on top of previous crystals.

3. Make a mass of crystals by pouring the saturated salt solution into a clear container. Let it slowly evaporate. Crystals will grow on the sides of the container.

PROTOCOL

STEP 1: First make a seed crystal by pouring a small amount of saturated salt solution onto a saucer or shallow bowl. As the liquid evaporates, crystals will start to form, usually overnight. Select a single square crystal and remove it from the dish.

STEP 2: Carefully pour the saturated salt solution into a clean container (making sure no undissolved salt gets in), allow the solution to cool, and then hang the seed crystal with string in the solution from a pencil or knife placed across the top of the container. You could cover the container with a coffee filter or paper towel to keep out dust yet permit evaporation.

STEP 3: Set the container in a location where it can remain undisturbed. You are more likely to get a perfect crystal instead of a mass of crystals if you allow the crystal to grow slowly (cooler temperature, shaded location) in a place free of vibrations. It can take a week or more to get a big crystal.

THE SCIENCE BEHIND THE FUN

The hardest part of this experiment is tying the thread around your seed crystal. But without the seed crystal, it's hard to get much more than crusty salt. The perfect seed crystal gives the extra salt in your solution perfect little places to attach to, and this is what will keep the crystal structure growing. This is the crystal lattice we discussed earlier. Salt has a perfectly cubic crystal lattice. It measures the same distance on all sides, no matter how big or small.

Salt is pretty simple. It has one sodium atom (Na) and one chlorine atom (Cl), clustered together over and over, to form a salt molecule. Thus the formula for salt is easy: NaCl. In the crystal lattice, the atoms repeat in every direction. Where there is a Cl atom showing, an Na atom can attach, and vice versa.

Salt is mined in many ways. In some places, solar evaporation of salt water produces salt crystals. There are also underground mines in salt domes where miners scoop up salt crystals or cut slabs of hardened salt into blocks. Some specialty shops sell salt from all over the world, which shows that salt is still an important part of our diet.

CRUSTY CRYSTALS

Create your own crystals around whatever structure you think up.

MATERIALS

- Pipe cleaners
- 1-quart (946 ml) wide-mouth glass Mason jar
- 12" (30 cm) string or fishing line
- Scissors
- Ruler, pencil, or single chopstick
- 1 quart (946 ml) of water
- Borax, sugar, or salt
- Long wooden spoon for stirring
- Blue (or another color) food coloring

PROTOCOL

STEP 1: Using pipe cleaners, create a framework of any shape—snowflake, square, pyramid, circle, etc.

STEP 2: Make sure that the shape can easily fit through the mouth of the wide-mouthed jar without having to squeeze through. If it can't, trim the sides down.

STEP 3: Cut a 6" (15 cm) length of string and attach it to one side of your pipe cleaner shape. Tie the other end of the string to a ruler, pencil, or chopstick. Make sure your framework hangs into the jar but doesn't come close to touching the bottom (leave about an inch [2.5 cm] of room). Once you have your length set, tie the knots and remove the shape from the jar.

Safety Tips

- Wash your hands after working with Borax.

- Ask an adult for help boiling the water.

- Be cautious around the stove to avoid burns.

STEP 4: Bring a pot with about a quart (946 ml) of water to a boil and pour about 3 cups (709 ml) of the hot liquid into the jar. Add 3 tablespoons (54 g) of Borax, sugar, or salt per each cup (235 ml) of water, so about 9 tablespoons (162 g) of one of these for a full jar. Stir it up, but don't worry if some Borax, sugar, or salt settles to the bottom of the jar.

STEP 5: If you want a colored crystal cluster, stir in some food coloring. You will have a little trouble seeing your shape as the crystals grow on it if you use a lot of food coloring. Now pour the mixture into the jar.

STEP 6: Use the string to hang the pipe cleaner framework in the jar, with the stick resting on top of the jar. Make sure that you've added enough solution to completely submerge the pipe cleaner.

STEP 7: Put the jar somewhere where it is safe from being disturbed. Leave it alone and let the science work without bumping it.

STEP 8: If you used Borax, you should have a nice cluster of crystals everywhere on the framework, and even on the string, by the next day. Sugar will take a little longer, and salt is the slowest (it could take two or three days).

 Creative Enrichment

1. Try twisting your pipe cleaners into flowers, snowflakes, or other forms.

THE SCIENCE BEHIND THE FUN

When you mixed the dry chemical with the water, you created a super-saturated suspension. A *suspension* is a mixture that contains solid particles large enough to settle out. By mixing the chemical into hot water, instead of room temperature or cold water, it stays suspended longer. If you used colder water, you would not be able to add as much dry chemical before it began to settle.

As the liquid begins to cool, it starts to crystallize. You'll see this crystallization on both the bottom of the

jar and on your pipe cleaner. The solution continues to make a crust on top of your framework and on top of other crystals until you pull it out of the water.

Borax, also known as sodium tetraborate, is a term for a common salt with the formula $Na_2B_4O_7 \cdot 10H_2O$. The B is for *boron*. Borax forms from evaporation of boron-rich waters, especially seasonal lakes, such as in Southern California and Nevada deserts.

LAB 4

GEODES OF FUN

Make a cluster of geodes from common kitchen chemicals. This experiment calls for alum, but you can use Borax in the same proportions as the Crusty Crystals lab on page 18, or use salt in the same proportion as in the Salty Squares lab on page 16.

MATERIALS

- Plastic eggs or small plastic bowls
- 1 quart (946 ml) of boiling water
- Mixing bowl or 1-quart (946 ml) wide-mouth glass Mason jar
- 2$\frac{1}{2}$ tablespoons (45 g) of pure alum powder (potassium aluminum sulfate—you must have the right kind!)
- Long wooden spoon for stirring
- Set of food coloring
- Superglue—don't use water-soluble glues

Safety Tips

- Avoid getting solutions in your eyes.

- Wash hands after using the chemicals.

- Ask an adult for help boiling the water.

- Be cautious around the cooking stove to avoid burns.

PROTOCOL

STEP 1: Make sure your plastic bowls or plastic eggs are clean. Note that you can also use actual eggshells if they are large enough, and *very* clean. Then you can break them away when you're done if your crystals are thick enough.

STEP 2: Bring a quart (946 ml) of water to a boil and pour about 3 cups (709 ml) of the hot liquid into a mixing bowl or Mason jar. Add 2$\frac{1}{2}$ tablespoons (45 g) of alum per each cup of water, so if you want to make a lot of geodes, keep that ratio. Stir it up, but don't worry if some alum settles to the bottom of the jar.

STEP 3: If you want a colored crystal cluster, stir in plenty of food coloring.

STEP 4: Put a few drops of glue in the bowl or egg, coating the inside edge. Before it dries, sprinkle in some alum, Borax, or salt crystals. These are the seed crystals that will help the geode grow faster.

STEP 5: Pour the mix into the plastic bowls or eggs. If you're using eggs, use a towel, a muffin tin, or empty egg container to hold the eggs upright.

STEP 6: Put the cooling forms somewhere where they are safe from spills.

STEP 7: After twenty-four hours, you should see a crust forming. It will take some time for all the water to evaporate, but if you don't want to wait that long, you can pour the remaining liquid into a jar and reuse it for more fun later.

 Creative Enrichment

1. Add fluorescent, glowing paint to your mix if you want to create a "space rock" effect.

THE SCIENCE BEHIND THE FUN

Geodes form in igneous and sedimentary rocks as hollow, round structures. They may begin as large bubbles or holes in the rock. Hot, quartz-rich fluids in the rocks can then reach the bubbles and start filling them in. Sometimes the hot fluids pick up colors from the rocks around them and leave colored agate bands inside the geodes.

Geodes often look like ordinary rocks on the outside. Because they cool slowly and evenly, crystals can form into fantastic shapes on the inside. The geodes also get refreshed with new surges of hot liquid, usually quartz, but other minerals, such as calcite, may come in. Sometimes the new material comes into the geode as a gas, so each crystal clinging to the inside of the geode can grow a little. Other times, the material comes in as a liquid, and the geode fills up with bands, from the bottom up.

Geodes and "thundereggs" are common in many parts of the U.S. where there is lots of lava, such as at Oregon's famed Richardson's Ranch. Keokuk, Iowa, is also known by rock hounds for its geodes. Cracking open a geode is a lot of fun, because you never know what's inside. There are many different websites where you can order your own geodes to break apart.

SPECIMENS, LAVA, AND SEDIMENTS

Now that we understand a little about minerals in their crystalline form, we'll turn to some of the ways that the Earth uses minerals to create new rocks.

Igneous rocks are the most dramatic way the Earth builds up its crust, usually in the form of lava flows and ash clouds. Geologists refer to lava as an *extrusive* rock, because it moved from inside the Earth to outside. Thus, extrusive rocks came out of the Earth. We'll talk later about the other kind of igneous rock, *intrusive* rocks that cool before they erupt from inside the Earth.

There are three main kinds of lava: basaltic, andesitic, and rhyolitic. *Basaltic* lava can be runny and form long flows that cover hundreds of miles or fill in gullies and valleys and end up several hundred feet thick. *Andesitic* lava tends to build up mountains, like in the Andes chain of South America. *Rhyolitic* lava is sometimes explosive, forming dangerous eruptions. All three help build up the Earth, but at this stage, you can use the term *lava* to mean simply "hot, flowing rock."

While igneous rocks can form in spectacular ways, most of the Earth's crust is covered with sedimentary rocks. Sedimentary rocks are named for the tiny bits of rock and mud—sediments—that build up when material settles out of water, including giant freshwater lakes and long, meandering rivers or active bays, lagoons, and straits in the deep ocean. Sometimes the water is muddy, and over the years, layer after layer of silt may settle out in a bay. Over lots of time, that *mudstone* can build up to thousands of feet or meters. Or a river may empty into the ocean and bring in lots of sand and rocks, creating *sandstone*. Elsewhere, a body of water may be carrying a lot of lime (calcium carbonate), building up until the water simply can't absorb any more chemicals. At that point, a *limestone* may start forming.

BUBBLE TROUBLE

Learn how to make rocks fizzle. This is the classic "acid on limestone" test used in laboratories and field kits all over the world.

MATERIALS

- Lab notebook and pen or pencil
- Chalk—blackboard chalk is best, rather than sidewalk chalk
- Small plates or bowls, at least 4
- Lemon juice
- pH testing strips
- Medicine dropper or small spoon
- Magnifying glass or hand lens (optional)
- Vinegar

PROTOCOL

STEP 1: Create a table or grid in your lab notebook to record your observations.

STEP 2: Put a small chunk of chalk in each bowl, all roughly equal in size.

STEP 3: Test the lemon juice for pH and record the results.

STEP 4: Add a few drops of lemon juice to a chalk sample and check for a reaction. Record your results. You may need a hand lens to view the reaction.

STEP 5: Test your vinegar for pH and record the results.

 Safety Tips

- Avoid getting vinegar or lemon juice in your eyes. Rinse thoroughly with cold water if you do.

- Do not breathe in the fumes that result from the chemical reaction.

STEP 6: Add a few drops of vinegar to a chalk sample and check for a reaction. Again, use a hand lens to check the surface of the sample, if necessary. Record your results.

STEP 7: Repeat steps 4 and 6, but this time, crush the chalk into a powder first.

 Creative Enrichment

1. If you have a piece of limestone, test it as a sample, and crushed up, with your two acids.

2. Try other rocks, such as dolomite and calcite.

3. Vary the temperature of the acid to see if that makes a difference.

4. Try different citrus fruit juices, testing each for pH and building on your grid.

5. Try grinding up a seashell and testing that.

THE SCIENCE BEHIND THE FUN

This experiment tests the science of chemical weathering, a significant force at the surface of the Earth. Your testing showed the relationship between pH and calcium carbonate, which is present in chalk, limestone, calcite, dolomite, and other carbonate-rich rocks. The fizzing you saw was a result of acetic acid (in the vinegar) and citric acid (in the lemon juice) attacking the carbonate, which is one carbon atom and three oxygen atoms: CO_3. When one of the oxygen atoms is removed, you create carbon dioxide: CO_2.

Acetic acid and citric acid are very weak, and thus safe for kids to use. College geology students studying mineralogy use hydrochloric acid (HCl) to perform these tests, resulting in a much more vigorous reaction. Field geologists often carry a small bottle of hydrochloric acid with them to test for limestone or dolomite. Limestone will actively bubble, while dolomite may require crushing or heated acid to produce a reaction. Common rocks such as quartz, agate, or basalt will not produce a reaction as they have no calcium carbonate.

Most surface water is slightly acidic and will slowly react with limestone and eat it away. This is why we see caverns in many large limestone formations. By constantly washing through the limestone, water can slowly dissolve the rock. The water then often carries so much liquid limestone that it will pick up the calcium carbonate and move it, creating stalactites, stalagmites, flowstones, and other formations.

CRYSTAL GEOMETRY

Learn how to determine a crystal's angle. You can even use the crystals that you made in Unit 1.

MATERIALS

- Ruler
- Protractor
- Crystal samples, such as quartz, pyrite, calcite, feldspar, mica, or the alum and other crystals you made in Unit 1
- Lab notebook and pen or pencil
- Hand lens (optional)

Safety Tips

- Avoid sharp edges on crystal faces.

PROTOCOL

STEP 1: Build a *goniometer* by placing the ruler at the center of the protractor, with 2 inches (5 cm) of the ruler extending below the protractor.

STEP 2: Place your crystal sample with one face along the bottom of the protractor, and one face along the ruler, so that you can measure one of the angles.

Creative Enrichment

1. What other minerals around the house can you measure?

2. How can you measure pictures of crystals you find online?

3. A material such as obsidian has no crystal structure. Do you know why?

STEP 3: Record the various angles until you have a full set of measurements.

STEP 4: Repeat for different crystals, until you have built a full table.

THE SCIENCE BEHIND THE FUN

The goniometer dates back to 1538, when it was described by Dutch mathematician Gemma Frisius, who was studying navigation and surveying. One of his students was Gerardus Mercator, who made a famous early map of the Earth called the Mercator Projection. Nobel prize–winning German physicist Max von Laue used a goniometer in 1912 to explore the atomic structure of crystals. Crystals have a distinctive, measurable angle to their appearance. No matter the size of the specimen, if you can measure its angles, those numbers should be the same whether the sample is as big as your hand or as small as your thumb.

Once you practice how to measure crystal angles, you can start to identify them by eye, without using a tool. For example, pure calcite crystals form a slightly tilted cube called a rhombohedron, with four angles on each two-dimensional face: 74 degrees, 106 degrees, 74 degrees, and 106 degrees, which add up to 360 degrees. Salt forms a perfect cube, with four angles of 90 degrees.

The next step is to learn to identify crystal habits—the common form a mineral adopts. There are seven common crystal habits: cubic, tetragonal, hexagonal, trigonal, orthorhombic, monoclinic, triclinic, and amorphous (no crystal structure, like glass). Once you start making a list of all the angles that you learn, you'll start to memorize them and then recognize them when you see them in the field. Geologists and mineralogists learn the angles and spot them even under a hand lens.

INTRIGUING INTRUSIONS

This experiment shows how granite rises. When lava doesn't break through the Earth's surface, it cools slowly. We'll see how that intrusion gradually rises over time, like you would see in a lava lamp.

MATERIALS

- 1-pint (473 ml) wide-mouth glass Mason jar (or a drinking glass will work)
- 1 cup (235 ml) of water, room temperature
- Food coloring (optional)
- ¼ cup (60 ml) of inexpensive vegetable oil
- 1 teaspoon of salt (big, coarse rock salt works great)

PROTOCOL

STEP 1: Add 1 cup (235 ml) of water to your Mason jar.

STEP 2: Add four or five drops of food coloring and stir it in. This is optional, but it helps you see what's going on.

STEP 3: Add the oil into the jar. As you probably know, oil floats on top of water.

STEP 4: Sprinkle the salt into your mixture. It should drop to the bottom.

 ## Creative Enrichment

1. Can you guess how much salt you could add before the mixture becomes super-saturated? Think back to the Salty Squares lab.

2. Does it matter what kind of oil you use?

 ### Safety Tips

- Avoid getting salt into your eyes.

- Don't knock over your jar.

THE SCIENCE BEHIND THE FUN

This simple take on a "lava lamp" is a little different from the original. The original uses a heat source that melts wax, which rises, cools, falls, and recycles itself. Other forms of this experiment use a lot more oil and effervescent tablets, such as Alka Seltzer, instead of salt. But they work on the same principle. There is a difference between the specific density of water and the specific density of vegetable oil. Most cooking oils measure about 0.92 g/cm³. Pure water is defined as 1.0 g/cm³. Since lighter fluids float on heavier fluids, the oil floats on top.

As you added the salt, it captured some oil on its way through the oil layer. This is because the surface tension of oil is high, so it wants to coat things, which you see as the mass drops through the oil. Once the salt reaches the bottom of the container, it starts to dissolve into the water, and as it dissolves, it releases the oil it captured. The oil then wants to rise above the water, and does so as an interesting bubble.

The difference in density is the same process that intrusions use to rise through the Earth's crust. They are just a little less dense than the material they are in, and hotter, so they rise slowly. Sometimes there may not be enough difference between the intrusion and the surrounding rock, so the hot magma eventually hardens in place, well below the surface. After a million years of erosion, or thanks to a continued push below, the granite eventually begins to poke out and form mountains.

COCOA CRUST

Instead of just making hot cocoa on a cold winter day, make a model of how the Earth's crust moves around thanks to heat from inside the planet.

MATERIALS

- 1 quart (946 ml) of heavy cream
- Medium cooking pot
- 1 cup (86 g) of powdered cocoa

Safety Tips

- Be cautious around the cooking stove to avoid burns.
- Ask an adult for help using the stove.

PROTOCOL

STEP 1: Pour the heavy cream into a medium cooking pot.

STEP 2: Cover the cream with a layer of cocoa, the thicker the better—close to ¼" (6 mm). Make the edges around the pan walls slightly thicker. You just created a model of a "super-continent."

STEP 3: Turn on the heat and slowly bring the cream to a boil.

STEP 4: Watch where cracks form as the system gets hotter, and imagine how many earthquakes you could feel if you were standing on such a piece of the crust. See if you can predict which cracks will grow the biggest.

STEP 5: Keep heating, and avoid the temptation to stir. By the end of the experiment, you may be down to one remaining "island" of crust.

STEP 6: Don't waste the ingredients! Add a little sugar to make hot chocolate.

Creative Enrichment

1. What happens if you make the chocolate layer $\frac{1}{2}''$ (1 cm) thick? Or use instant hot cocoa mix?

2. What happens if you use milk instead of cream?

THE SCIENCE BEHIND THE FUN

The interior of our planet is very hot—probably over 9,032°F (5,000°C) at the inner core, and ranging from 2,912°F to 6,692°F (1,600°C to 3,700°C) in the mantle. With all that heat and pressure, the rocks in the mantle don't behave much like rocks; they're more like plastic or toothpaste. That heat at the core of the Earth must go somewhere, however, and scientists believe it swirls around in currents through the mantle, just like the heat from the stove moved the heavy cream around.

As the heat increases, the currents in the cream scrape away at the chocolate layer that represents the Earth's crust, and finally, you started to see cracks begin. Wherever the crust was thin, the boiling cream found the weakness. At the end, you may even see the "plates" start to rock as the heat shifts them. At the Earth's surface, there are several rift zones where the rocks are pulling away from each other. These are *divergent* boundaries or zones where the crust is expanding. You should have also seen a "triple junction" where there were three lines of weakness and, eventually, the cream broke through. You could imagine that being a small shield volcano if the cocoa layer was hard enough for the cream to build up.

The theory of continental drift, also called plate tectonics, was first advanced by Dr. Alfred Wegener in 1912. However, it wasn't accepted until the 1960s.

FUN WITH MUD

It may look like dirty water, but you'd be surprised how much is floating in there.

MATERIALS

- 1 quart (1 liter) of soil, dug from the garden—don't use store-bought potting soil
- Bucket and shovel
- Lab notebook and pen or pencil
- Scale (optional)
- Large, wide-mouth jar with lid
- 1 quart (946 ml) of water
- Long stick or paint mixer (optional)
- Screen or strainer (optional)
- Set of bowls (optional)

 Safety Tips

- Avoid spills.

- Be careful where you dig to get your soil sample. Get permission first.

Creative Enrichment

1. If you have a set of screens with big and little holes, keep going in this lab by dumping the contents into a tub and separating out the material. Put sticks, leaves, and other organic material in a container and put big rocks in another. Then measure out how much sand and clay you have and calculate the ratios.

2. Try the lab again, using a soil sample from another location.

3. Remember these skills for the Building Bricks lab on page 72.

PROTOCOL

STEP 1: Collect your soil sample. Record the experience in your lab book: what you did, what colors you saw, how hard was it to shovel out, etc. You can find the weight of your sample by weighing the empty bucket first, then the bucket with soil, and subtracting the bucket's weight to find the final weight.

STEP 2: Fill your jar halfway with the soil you collected.

STEP 3: Add water almost to the top of the jar and put the lid on.

STEP 4: Shake up the jar and break up the clumps. You might want to take the lid off and reach in with a long stick to help things along. A long wooden stick used to mix paint works.

STEP 5: Return the lid and shake it up some more, then let it settle overnight. When you return, make notes about what you see. How did the material settle?

THE SCIENCE BEHIND THE FUN

Soil types depend on how much sand, clay, and organic material is present. Soil scientists do not use the word *dirt*. They either use the word *soil* or they use even more precise terms, like sandy loam and *alluvium*. By noting how much of each main ingredient is present, scientists can tell gardeners and farmers how to treat their soil with the right fertilizer. One handy tool they use is the Silt-Sand-Clay triangle, based on those ratios.

Did you find many big rocks in your sample? Chances are that you didn't. Gardeners like to remove big rocks. How about sand? Was there very much sand in your sample? Usually there is, and you can divide up the sand particles into fine, very fine, coarse, and very coarse. Measuring the size of the sand is usually something you need many specialized screens for, but it is

an important thing to know if you are a soil scientist. The first scale for classifying sediment sizes was developed by American sedimentary scientist J.A. Udden, and was adapted by C.K. Wentworth in 1922.

SEDIMENT SIZES	
Type	**Size**
Clay	0.0001–0.002 mm
Silt	0.002–0.05 mm
Sand	0.05–2 mm
Granule	2–4 mm ($\frac{8}{100}$"–$\frac{2}{10}$")
Pebble	4–64 mm ($\frac{2}{10}$"–$2\frac{1}{2}$")
Cobble	64–256 mm ($2\frac{1}{2}$"–10")
Boulder	256 mm (10")

TASTY CONGLOMERATE

Make sedimentary rocks with your favorite ingredients. This is a *conglomerate*—a collection of bits and pieces of material all glued together.

MATERIALS

- Mixing bowl
- 2 cups (312 g) of oats
- 1 cup (25 g) of puffed rice cereal, such as Rice Krispies
- ½ cup (50 g) of pretzels, chopped up
- ¼ cup (42 g) of tiny candy shell–covered chocolates, such as M&M's Minis
- Medium saucepan
- ¼ cup (55g) of butter
- ¼ cup (85 g) of honey
- ¼ cup (65 g) of creamy peanut butter
- ¼ cup (60 g) of brown sugar
- Wooden spoon or firm rubber spatula
- 1 teaspoon (5 ml) of vanilla extract
- Glass baking dish
- Parchment paper

Safety Tips
- Be careful with glass mixing bowls.
- Ask an adult for help using the stove.

PROTOCOL

STEP 1: In a large bowl, mix your oats, puffed rice, pretzels, and mini candies. Note that the ingredients list can vary depending on what you like—you can substitute cashews, raisins, chocolate chips, bigger candies, etc. Just keep the proportions about the same. This mixture will be your *clasts*.

STEP 2: In a medium saucepan, melt the "glue" for your conglomerate. Add the butter, honey, peanut butter, and brown sugar and bring it to a boil. Stir continuously so it doesn't stick. Reduce the heat and let it simmer for three minutes and keep stirring. Remove from the heat and add the vanilla.

STEP 3: Add the glue, or *matrix*, to your clasts in the large mixing bowl and stir together until you have everything distributed throughout the mixture.

STEP 4: Line the glass baking dish with parchment paper and add your mixture. Pack it down with your wooden spoon or rubber spatula so that it is nice and flat and even. You can add more candy, raisins, nuts, etc., at this point, either sprinkling them on top or pushing them in slightly.

STEP 5: Put in the refrigerator for about ten minutes, then remove and cut into squares or rectangles. Enjoy!

Creative Enrichment

1. Is it possible to have too many pieces of candy?

THE SCIENCE BEHIND THE FUN

Conglomerates are common sedimentary rocks. They are usually composed of rounded pebbles of various sizes but at least 2 mm ($\frac{5}{64}$") in diameter or else they're just coarse sandstone. Sometimes conglomerates are glued together with such a hard, lime-rich matrix that they are very hard to break apart. Other times, they have way more rocky material (clasts) than they do matrix, and they crumble apart easily.

It takes very strong water current to move big rocks, and the size of the rocks in a conglomerate tells geolo-gists a few things about where the conglomerate was made. If the pebbles and cobbles are not very eroded, they will still have sharp angles and corners, and the resulting rock is called a *breccia*. This usually means that the rocks have not traveled very far, and the water current when they were laid down was not very strong.

Gold miners often have to break up conglomerates to wash the gold out. Generally, the bigger the rocks in a stream, the bigger the gold. Conglomerates with large rocks in gold country are often a good sign!

METAMORPHOSIS AND BREAKDOWN

In the labs so far, we have learned about the two main ways that new rocks form, through fire and water. But there is a third type of rock: *metamorphic*. These rocks start out as a volcano or a sediment, but undergo so much "cooking" deep inside the Earth that they change. Sometimes they change in profound and interesting ways from pressure and heat.

Closer to the surface, every rock and cliff faces big challenges every day, from sun, air, water, plants, and gravity.

You may not have thought about the Earth being an efficient recycler, but it is. In these labs, we'll learn how the Earth is always trying to recycle its rocks. Scientists use the term *entropy* to measure how fast things fall apart. It is the nature of all things to eventually break down and disappear; mountains rise and fall, plants and animals grow and die. Some processes occur quickly, out in the open, and some occur slowly, hidden from sight. In these labs, you'll learn why it is inevitable that rocks fall apart.

SNAKY SCHIST

If sedimentary rocks are generally flat when they are laid down, how did they get so wavy?

MATERIALS

- 4 slices of yellow cheddar cheese at room temperature
- 4 slices of white cheddar cheese at room temperature

Safety Tips

- Don't make a mess with your cheese, but in this lab, it's okay to play with your food!

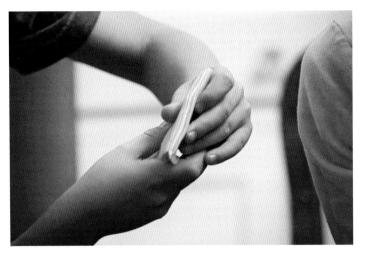

PROTOCOL

STEP 1: Take your slices of cheese from the refrigerator. Alternate colors of cheese to neatly stack five slices. Push the edges slightly so a rise appears in the middle. This is an *anticline*. If the bulge dipped down, you would have a *syncline*.

STEP 2: Take your stack apart and put three slices into one neat pile and the other two, plus one new slice, into another. Put the second stack in the refrigerator.

STEP 3: Holding the edges straight, make folds in the cheese by pushing the edges together a little bit at a time. You should see a mound form much easier this time. See how far it can bend without breaking.

STEP 4: Remove the second stack from the refrigerator and immediately repeat the experiment. Don't let the cheese warm up.

STEP 5: Make cheese sandwiches from your leftovers. Making grilled cheese sandwiches will turn the cheese into a metamorphic rock!

 Creative Enrichment

1. Use a thermometer to record the actual temperature of your cheese samples.

2. What would happen if you spread mayonnaise between your layers before you start folding?

3. Try freezing your cheese and see if you can make a single fold. Some rocks are so brittle they don't fold—they fracture.

THE SCIENCE BEHIND THE FUN

When layers of rock get buried at great depths, they stop acting like rocks and start acting like, well, melted cheese. You can see how much easier it is to create folds when there is plenty of heat, because the cheese was much easier to bend. As the heat increases, you can almost fold your cheese layers like an accordion.

It should be easier for you to understand what happens not only to rocks the size of your cheese sample, but also to giant slabs of rocks that are heated up and pushed around. Geologists can tell how much heat and pressure a rock has been through by the minerals they find. If a rock gets more heat and pressure, it will become a slate, a common metamorphic rock. It may have started out as a mudstone but has hardly undergone any metamorphism. The next step is phyllite, and then schist. Finally, the rocks become gneiss, which is very hard.

More Heat and Pressure

Mud → Mudstone → Slate → Phyllite → Schist → Gneiss

LAB 12

CHOCOLATE ROCK CYCLE

Use chocolate to learn about all the different rock cycles.

MATERIALS

- Block or chips of dark chocolate
- Kitchen grater
- Aluminum foil
- Small pot
- 2 cups (475 ml) water
- 4–5 paper cupcake holders
- Block or chips of white chocolate
- Chocolate syrup (optional)

 Safety Tips

- Be careful around a hot stove.

- Ask an adult for help using the stove.

- Don't hurt your fingers when you grate up the chocolate.

PROTOCOL

STEP 1: Start by making some "sedimentary" chocolate rock. Take a block of dark chocolate, or large chips—which you can think of as cooled "metamorphic" rock. Use a grater to grate about ¼ cup (44 g) of chocolate powder. This is like the effects of erosion, creating dry sand or mud—the basics of a sedimentary rock.

STEP 2: Create a small "boat" out of aluminum foil and place the powder inside it. Now float the boat in a small pot of water over low heat until you see the powder melt into a liquid chocolate lava flow. This is now "igneous" chocolate.

STEP 3: Pour the hot liquid chocolate lava into a paper cupcake holder and let it cool.

STEP 4: Once cool, break the chocolate into pieces, the way mountains break apart due to erosion. Grate some small shavings from the white chocolate, add it to the broken chocolate pieces, and sprinkle in some chocolate chips if you want. You can add some chocolate syrup, too.

STEP 5: Place the mixture of different types of chocolate "rocks" in a small square of aluminum foil, about 8″ x 8″ (20 x 20 cm). Fold the aluminum foil up by half several times until the chocolate is safely wrapped inside. You can also use sturdy resealable plastic bags.

STEP 6: Place the foil on a flat surface and push on it, but don't use too much force or you could break open the foil. You want enough pressure to press the chocolate particles together—like the amount of force needed to create metamorphic rocks. A light tap with a rubber mallet or a rolling pin would also work.

STEP 7: Carefully unwrap the foil and check out the result. You should see a "chocolate schist." By applying a little pressure, and some heat from friction, you forced the chocolate particles to compress together into a metamorphic rock again.

Creative Enrichment

1. What could you do next to the "metamorphic" chocolate to re-start the cycle?

THE SCIENCE BEHIND THE FUN

Congratulations! You just made a complete cycle through the three main rock types. There is no way to say for sure where rocks start in their journey, so we arbitrarily started with a metamorphic rock and began eroding it. Next, we melted the sedimentary rock and formed volcanic chocolate lava, then we mashed it all together like a metamorphic rock. If your mixture was hard enough, you could start over and begin grating it back into a fine powder. The Earth is a great at recycling rocks. That's the way it happens in the Earth's crust: rocks go through a journey from one form to the next. That's why we say that the Earth is geologically active—these processes are going on all the time.

SUNNY EXPOSURE

Watch the sun's rays fade images and make things look old. What happens if the sun bakes a cliff all day, every day, for millions of years?

MATERIALS

- **Masking tape**
- **Cookie cutters, in various shapes and sizes. You can also use leaves, but you'll have to use tape on their back side to keep them from moving.**
- **Several different types of paper—newsprint, magazine pages, common printer paper, etc. If you can find sun-sensitive paper, that's the best to use, but it can be hard to find.**
- **Lab notebook and pen or pencil**

 Safety Tips

- Avoid direct exposure to the sun for prolonged periods, and always wear sunscreen—even on cloudy days!

- Watch out for hot surfaces.

PROTOCOL

STEP 1: Use masking tape to cover the cookie cutters so that the whole image acts as a stencil.

STEP 2: Place your different sheets of paper outdoors, then arrange the cookie cutter images so that you still have lots of paper exposed. If it's windy, you may also perform this experiment indoors on a windowsill, but direct sunlight is best. If you use photographic paper, keep it upside down until the last moment.

STEP 3: Note the time, and begin regular observations. Do not move the cookie cutters around, or else you will blur the lines. When you first begin, you might want to make predictions about which kinds of paper will react faster in direct sunlight.

STEP 4: After six hours, remove the cookie cutters and observe what is happening to the exposed paper and the unexposed paper. Take notes on color, how much sun is out, length of time, etc. If you used photographic paper, you won't have to wait that long.

STEP 5: Continue exposing the paper to the sun as long as you'd like—up to three or four days, or even more. How did your predictions come out?

 Creative Enrichment

1. Tape different materials over the cookie cutters and determine what effect they have.

2. Try as many different kinds of paper as you can find.

THE SCIENCE BEHIND THE FUN

The sun not only beams light down on the surface of the Earth, but it also releases ultra-violet rays. Anyone who has had the misfortune of getting a sunburn knows just how relentless those rays are. Your skin has no good defenses unless you have a lot of pigmentation, and even that is not protection for most of us.

There are two ways that the sun helps break down rocks. First, there is heat. Under the rays of the sun, rocks tend to build up heat to a point where they can be hot enough to cause blisters when picked up. Heated rocks tend to expand, which can produce tiny cracks. When rocks heat up during the day and cool off at night, this results is a kind of push-pull effect

where the rocks expand and contract continually, which can break down the chemical bonds that make rock-forming minerals.

Second, the streaming UV rays start a chemical reaction on many of the materials they reach. Combined with the tendency of water in the air to help oxidize materials, sun rays break down molecules and immediately begin to "age" whatever they touch. Like the paper you used in your experiment, the sun may dry out material, turn it different colors, or even burn off chemicals. The result is that the sun tends to age whatever it touches, and, while slow, it is still effective over millions of years.

SHAKE AND BREAK

Rocks are very strong, but they can't last forever when they get rolled, shaken, stirred, and jumbled. In this lab, you'll mimic the forces that break rocks down into sand, and have a sweet time doing it.

MATERIALS

- **5 sheets of 8½″ x 11″ (21.5 x 28 cm) paper**
- **Pen or pencil**
- **2 boxes of sugar cubes**
- **Kitchen scale**
- **Hard plastic container with lid**
- **Selection of small pebbles. You can also use split shot fishing weights.**

Safety Tips

- Don't use a glass jar— it could break.

- Keep the lid on tight.

- Wash hands after touching the sugar so you don't make a mess or get it into your eyes.

PROTOCOL

STEP 1: Take a blank piece of paper and divide it into four quarters, or quadrants. Label the quadrants Boulder, Cobble, Pebble, Sand.

STEP 2: Place sixteen cubes on the scale and weigh them. Record the weight on your sheet of paper.

STEP 3: Place the sugar cubes in the container, put the lid on tightly, and shake vigorously for one minute.

STEP 4: Dump the contents onto your sheet of paper and divide up the material. The largest chunks are probably boulders, and the finest material is sand. If you have tiny chunks of sugar that are almost broken up, call them pebbles. Cobbles would be the group that is too small to be a boulder and too large to be a pebble.

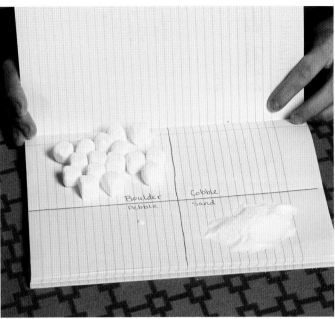

STEP 5: Weigh each section and create a table. Add up all of your measurements and see how close you get to the original weight.

STEP 6: Now vary your process. Try getting another person to shake the same number of cubes for one minute. Or you can repeat the test yourself and vary the time. Next, you can add a combination of rocks and pebbles or fishing weights and see if they change the way the sugar cubes break down.

 Creative Enrichment

1. How long do you think it would take for you to turn all the boulders into sand? Can you set up a contest with your friends and family?

2. What would happen if you put your sugar cubes in a smaller container, so that they don't have enough room to move around?

3. What happens if you put in the same volume of rocks and sugar?

THE SCIENCE BEHIND THE FUN

Mechanical forces that pit one rock against another are very common in the Earth's crust. When earthquakes move rocks over, under, or against each other, the result is often a pulverized powder. When rocks fall off a cliff and pile up below, the common term to refer to them is *scree*, as in a scree slope. Scree describes piles of rock that are mostly small. Geologists use the term *talus* (tay-lus) for slopes that are a jumble of large and small rock fragments. These may contain boulders the size of a car and are often not sorted very well,

comprising a mix of huge, big, and little rocks. Each time another rock comes flying down, it will hit other rocks and break things down further. As long as the cliff above continues to be attacked by gravity, wind, sun, tree roots, and water, the talus slope will continue to build. Sometimes that's good—you won't have to climb the cliff to look for samples or fossils if they are always raining down from above. Just be sure to wear a hardhat!

READING RUST

Show how even common substances can break down a strong material, like steel.

MATERIALS

- **3 pieces of steel wool**
- **3 plastic cups or shallow dishes**
- **Gloves**
- **Water**
- **1 tablespoon (18 g) of salt**

PROTOCOL

STEP 1: Place each piece of steel wool in a cup or shallow dish (wear gloves because steel wool can give splinters).

STEP 2: Pour equal amounts of water over two of the pieces of steel wool. Leave the third piece dry.

STEP 3: Sprinkle one of these wet pieces with plenty of salt.

STEP 4: Observe and compare the pieces every day for a week.

 Safety Tips

- Avoid getting any steel wool "dust" in your eyes or on your skin.

- Don't get salt in your eyes—use gloves.

Creative Enrichment

1. What happens if you use a copper scratch pad instead of steel wool?

2. What else can you use besides salt?

THE SCIENCE BEHIND THE FUN

This lab shows you the power of chemical weathering. Even though it's made of steel, the steel wool you used isn't that strong up against acids and salt. By the time you finished this lab, you probably had nothing left of the steel wool but a gooey mess.

When the steel wool got wet, the water got right to work attacking anyplace it could find on the surface of the steel fibers. Any spare oxygen gas in the water began to attach to electrons given off by the steel to form iron oxide. This is called *oxidation,* and it is a very powerful force. There are many forms of iron oxide, but its most common form is red rust, with the chemical formula Fe_2O_3. That means there are two iron atoms (Fe, from the Latin *ferrum*) and three oxygen atoms.

When you added salt into the mix, you sped up the oxidation process. The reason is that the electrons from the iron can move around even faster in salt water. Salt water is a very good conductor of electricity for the same reason.

During the winter, many areas use salt to melt snow and ice before it can build up and make roads danger-ous. You can now imagine the damage that salt would cause on the underside of your family's car. For that reason, some road crews use sand, cinders, or chemicals that are more environmentally friendly.

UNDERSTANDING THE EARTH

We started at the smallest scale, building up crystals and rocks and then breaking them back down. Now it's time to look at geology on a bigger scale. We live on a young planet; we know that because the continents are still moving, and volcanoes still erupt. Geologists believe that as planets get older, those forces stop. And yet it's an old planet as far as birthdays go—billions of years old.

In these labs, you'll get an understanding for just how old the Earth really is—measured in billions of years. You'll also learn how to mimic one of the most interesting geological events—the geyser. We will also look at all the different ways the Earth leaves us clues that we are not the only ones living here. You'll learn some of the different ways that the Earth creates fossils for us to enjoy.

LAB 16

MANY BIRTHDAYS

See just how old the Earth is and how hard it is to imagine the scale.

MATERIALS

- Old deck of cards
- Glue (staples also work)
- Coloring markers

PROTOCOL

STEP 1: Take an old deck of cards. Count out forty-five cards, which is all you'll need for this lab. Each card represents 100 million years, and you'll show how they correspond to the Earth's age, estimated at 4.54 billion years old.

STEP 2: Glue thirty-nine of those cards together into a single stack. Make it as straight as possible so the edges match up. Color these cards with brown edges. This group represents the *Precambrian* era—it covers the first 3.9 billion or so years of Earth.

STEP 3: Use a purple marker to color the edges of three cards. Glue them together and stack them on top of the brown cards. This represents the *Paleozoic* era. It lasted about 300 million years, so we round down to the nearest hundred-millionth place and use three cards.

STEP 4: Use a green marker to color the edge of two cards. This is the *Mesozoic* era, the age of dinosaurs. It lasted about 180 million years.

STEP 5: You have now accounted for all the time recognized by geologists except for the last 60 million years. You can round that up to 100 million years and place one final card on the top. Color it yellow.

 Creative Enrichment

1. Can you think of a way to break up the last 60 million years to show the relationship if humans have been on the Earth for about 4 million years?

THE SCIENCE BEHIND THE FUN

The Earth is really old—and not much is known about the early years. Geologists have used radioactive dating to measure the oldest rock known, a gneiss located in Canada, at about 3.9 billion years. The first thirty-nine cards in your lab deck represent a time on the Earth that we don't know much about. That's the brown zone of your deck. There aren't many rocks to study, so we have to make educated guesses about what the world was like.

By the time you get to the purple and green cards, we have more fossils to study and we know a lot more about the conditions then. But what about that yellow card for the most recent time? You could start over with sixty new cards, and color them to show the divisions that geologists use for the *Cenozoic* era. The current time is called the *Quaternary* period, and it started just 11,000 years ago.

LAB
17

GUSHING GEYSERS

The classic "Mentos in a soda bottle" experiment shows one way geysers can work.

MATERIALS

- 2-liter bottle of diet cola at room temperature
- Sheet of paper, rolled into a tube to hold the candies
- 7 Mentos candies

 Safety Tips

- Stand back! This lab can get messy!

- Avoid getting soda in your eyes.

PROTOCOL

STEP 1: Place the bottle of cola somewhere that is easy to wash down with a hose, such as a driveway.

STEP 2: Roll up the paper into a tube and insert the seven candies. Make sure the roll will guide the candies in quickly.

STEP 3: Place a finger over the bottom of the roll, and then position it over the soda bottle.

STEP 4: Release the candies and move away quickly

 Creative Enrichment

1. You can adjust many variables in this experiment—temperature, flavor, brand, number of candies, etc.—to see what produces the best geyser.

2. Check the surface of the candy with a hand lens—what does it look like? What would happen if you took fine sandpaper and smoothed out all those pits before you try this experiment?

THE SCIENCE BEHIND THE FUN

When you drop in your candy, the carbon dioxide in the soda is immediately attracted to the candy surface. Because of all those pits in the sugar, your candy has hundreds of places for the carbon dioxide to form bubbles. These are called *nucleation sites*. This is similar to the experiments you ran when you created crystals out of salt and sugar. Only instead of allowing the seed crystal to slowly build up the crystal structure, you are starting a violent reaction as more and more carbon dioxide releases from the diet soda. If the candy is smooth, there are far fewer places for the reaction to begin, and the results aren't as dramatic. Another factor to consider is the weight of the candies—they are heavy enough to sink in the soda bottle and find more carbon dioxide to liberate.

If you use plain soda water instead of diet cola, you also get less action. Diet drinks have less surface tension, thanks to the artificial sweeteners, so there is less force to hold the soda together. If you imagine a large chamber of hot magma just below the surface, when the pressure is suddenly released, you don't get lava—you get an eruption of ash. There is enough air rushing in to mix with the magma and it turns into an ash cloud, rather than a lava flow.

Real geysers, such as Old Faithful at Yellowstone National Park, operate somewhat differently. Hot groundwater in a large void heats up rapidly to a boil, and then begins to rise quickly. If you were to try to conduct an experiment like that, it would be very dangerous and not nearly as much fun.

PRESS A LEAF

Make an impression of a leaf—just like Mother Nature does.

MATERIALS

- ¼ cup (32 g) of cornstarch
- ½ cup (110 g) of baking soda
- ¼ cup (60 ml) of water
- Plate
- Wax paper
- Scissors
- 2-3 leaves or small branches; ginkgo and sequoia are excellent choices
- Diluted black watercolor paint

PROTOCOL

STEP 1: First, create your "fossil dough." Stir the cornstarch, baking soda, and water in a small saucepan and cook at medium heat until it forms a paste.

STEP 2: Remove from the stove and scrape it out onto a plate. After it cools, knead the dough as you would if you were baking bread.

STEP 3: Shape into six balls and put them in the refrigerator.

STEP 4: Cut six squares of wax paper, about 6″ x 6″ (15 x 15 cm).

STEP 5: Place a ball of dough on a wax paper square and smash it out so it is flat and round.

STEP 6: Press your plant material into the dough and remove it, leaving a fossil imprint.

STEP 7: When the dough dries, you can lightly paint your impression with diluted black water color—just enough to highlight it—or you can use more paint as you wish. If you find your dough cracks too much, you can simply use modeling clay.

Safety Tips

- Keep all materials out of your eyes.

Creative Enrichment

1. Look up the scientific name of the plant and label it in the dough by pressing with a toothpick tip.

2. What colors make the most realistic fossil?

THE SCIENCE BEHIND THE FUN

Most of the time when you collect plant fossils, you won't recover plant material. Unlike petrified wood, where the original chemicals have been replaced by quartz, a typical plant fossil is usually just an impression of the original. The black coloring that is common to plant fossils is usually some carbon that remained behind as the rest of the plant dissolved.

Gingkoes and sequoias are both a kind of "living fossil"—they are still around us after millions of years. The *metasequoia* is the state fossil of Oregon, but it's not very different from the sequoia trees that are common in California. If Oregon is cooler than California today but there are sequoia fossils in Oregon, what does that tell you about the climate when those sequoia fossils were laid down? It must have been a little warmer back then.

By studying leaves, seeds, wood, and other fossils, we can learn a lot about the climate when the fossils formed. Geologists who study fossils are called *paleontologists*, scientists who study ancient life. As you can probably guess, studying ancient life means you must know a lot about present-day life, too, so you can make comparisons. Paleontologists are very interested in evolution—how plants and animals have changed over time to adapt to the changing world around them. Ever since the Earth could sustain life, about 3.8 billion years ago, the fossil record has left us clues about the world back then. Sorting it all out is like solving a puzzle, but it's a lot of fun.

MAKE A MOLD

Create your own dinosaur footprint. If you don't want to create a dinosaur footprint, you can use any plastic animal or real seashell. But, come on, dinosaurs are more fun to play with.

MATERIALS

- Mold container (e.g., small plastic cap from a water bottle, tuna can, etc.)
- Small plastic sheets
- Pre-mixed spackling compound, plaster of Paris, or other clay
- Dinosaur toy with accurate feet
- Nonstick cooking spray

PROTOCOL

STEP 1: Make sure your plastic lid is clean.

STEP 2: Place a small square of plastic in the bottom of the lid so that you can remove the mold later.

STEP 3: Press in your clay, spackle, or other compound.

STEP 4: Spray the feet of your dinosaur toy with nonstick cooking oil. This will prevent any bits of clay from sticking to the toy.

STEP 5: Press the feet of the plastic dinosaur toy into the compound to make an impression. Make sure you get a strong, even impression. Check the dinosaur feet for bits of clay that still cling to the plastic; if you need to try again, you can spray more nonstick cooking oil lightly on the plastic and smooth out the clay to try again.

 Safety Tips

- Clay can make a mess—don't do this lab on a carpet!

STEP 6: Let the mold dry completely; then remove it from the plastic cap. You can trim the edges, paint it lightly with a water color, or coat it with shellac. You can also put it in a bezel or attach a hook to hang it as jewelry.

STEP 7: You can experiment with common lids you have around the house.

Creative Enrichment

1. How would you create a complete track, where the animal's footprints record it walking in a line for a distance?

2. Measure how big your foot is in relationship to how tall you are. How accurate is your model based on that math? If your dinosaur footprint were 7 feet (2 m) long, how big would the dinosaur be?

THE SCIENCE BEHIND THE FUN

If you've ever stepped in mud on a sunny day, you've made a mold of your footprint. If the mud were to dry hard after several days, that mold could last quite a while. Now just imagine if a storm rolled in and the area was severely flooded, with a new, thick layer of sand, silt, and clay covering your tracks. All you would need is more flooding, more burial, and if enough weight built up over it, the mud would turn to rock and preserve your footprint for a long, long time.

The first dinosaur tracks identified by scientists were found in 1802 in Massachusetts. However, Native Americans created *petroglyphs* near several rec-

ognized trackways in the western U.S., and these carvings translated to "location with bird tracks." The interesting thing is that the native people recognized the relationship between dinosaurs and birds long before paleontologists did.

Today, scientists can learn a lot about the dinosaur that laid down the tracks by measuring the depth of the imprint, the size of the track, and even the distance between tracks. There are places that seem to show a herd of dinosaurs all moving in a single direction, and there are sites that appear to show a predator chasing down their next meal.

PROSPECTING AND SPACE ROCKS

It's time to get out a magnifying glass or a hand lens and look closely at what prospectors call *black sands*. These are the tiny dark specks in sand that can sometimes hold the most value. They are often tiny slivers of magnetite, but they can also be particles of iron, silver, platinum, and even more exotic material. In rare cases, they may be star dust—tiny meteorites that fall to Earth. Tiny garnets are also common at the bottom of a gold pan.

Learning to identify and collect black sands can make you a good prospector. Any experienced gold panner will tell you that you always get black sands with gold, but you might not always get gold in your black sands. Another old saying that the prospectors shared was "gold is where you find it."

One thing about geology—for the rules to work here, they have to work everywhere. There's no such thing as "European geology" or "North American geology." The same rules are assumed to apply on Mars and the moon, and so far, they do. We know the moon has lots of lava flows, and we know Mars has lots of iron-rich red surface rocks. Rules, after all, are rules.

We are learning more every day about the role of comets and meteors in Earth processes, and it makes sense that there shouldn't be a lot of mystery there. They are, after all just rocks. Fancy rocks, but still, rocks. We'll look at some of the processes we believe are at work throughout the solar system and beyond. And we'll look at impact craters and play around with how they form.

FLASH IN THE PAN

Learn how to use a gold pan just like the old-timers.

MATERIALS

- Large, flat tub
- Soil or store-bought "pay dirt"
- Fishing weights, small lead split shots, or BBs
- Small gold pan—but a small aluminum pie pan will work

Safety Tips

- Avoid splashing muddy water into your eyes.

- Rubbing your fingers into sand and gravel can scrape away skin.

- Don't pan for too long at first—you can get some sore muscles in your wrists, arms, and shoulders, or in your thighs if you squat down too long.

PROTOCOL

STEP 1: Fill a large tub about three-quarters full of water. If you don't have a big tub, a 10-gallon (38 liter) cooler will work. Don't use the kitchen sink!

STEP 2: If you purchase some "salted" pay dirt online, you can use that for this step. If you live near gold country, such as the Mother Lode region of California, you could visit a river and bring home a sample. Barring all that, use ordinary soil.

STEP 3: Fill your gold pan about halfway full of soil and add in the weights or split shot, if you don't have actual pay dirt. These are your "nuggets" and flakes.

STEP 4: Dunk the pan into the water carefully so nothing flows out. With your fingers, break up any clumps of dirt or clay, and if any sticks or leaves float to the top, remove them.

STEP 5: Let some of the dirty water pour off, but just a little bit. Stir the pan again and make sure nothing is sticking to the bottom. Swirl it around and make sure everything is broken down. This is called a "slurry."

STEP 6: If your pan has riffles, make sure these are on the far side of the pan. Shuffle the pan carefully so that everything in the pan moves slightly away from you, with the pan tilted down so just a little bit washes across the riffles and out.

STEP 7: Bring the pan back to level and swirl it around several times, then tilt the pan away from you again and slide the slurry against your riffles. Let a little bit slop over the top, then re-settle and do that again and again. Feel around again and make sure everything is broken up, and pick out any large rocks. Make sure they are clean—sometimes gold can stick to rocks, so be sure they are washed.

STEP 8: Again and again, swirl the pan while it is level, and then slide the contents of the pan away from you and across the riffles. Wash against the riffles until the pan is nearly empty—do you see a flash in the pan?

 Creative Enrichment

1. Try another sample with the same weights in it and see how fast you can pan down to nothing but the lead shot.

THE SCIENCE BEHIND THE FUN

Gravity does your work for you when you use a gold pan. The old 49ers didn't have pans with riffles, so you have a big advantage, because the riffles create an eddy behind them and trap heavier particles under the lip. Every time you stop to resettle the contents in the pan, you do something scientific—you "re-stratify" the pan. All the heaviest material goes to the bottom, and all the lighter material rides to the top. This is because of three scientific principles—gravity, density, and water as a solvent. That's why every time you pan for gold, you are performing a science experiment!

Gold is one of the heaviest of all elements—19.3 grams per cubic centimeter, when pure. Check out the chart on the right for the density of other heavy metals.

HEAVY METALS	
Metal	Density (g/c³)
Gold	19.2
Tungsten	19.4
Uranium	20.2
Platinum	21.5
Iridium	22.4
Osmium	22.6

VUGS AND VEINS

Using cupcake mix and frosting, you can see how material is squeezed into the rocks in the Earth. And you can eat the result!

MATERIALS

- Cupcake mix
- Cupcake tin and paper cups
- Drinking glass
- Frosting (white or yellow)
- Frosting bag with nozzle
- Knife to cut the cupcakes in half

PROTOCOL

STEP 1: Prepare your cupcakes according to the recipe on a cake mix from the store or bake them from scratch. Don't make full-sized cupcakes—let them be about three-quarter size, or even half. If you're in a hurry, you can purchase cupcakes at the store, but look for smaller ones.

STEP 2: After the cupcakes have cooled, put one in the glass right side up and the other upside down so the sticky top layers meet. If you don't have smaller cupcakes, you can cut a big one in half.

 Safety Tips

- Be cautious around the oven to avoid burns.

- Ask an adult for help using the oven.

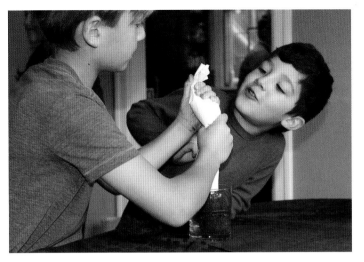

STEP 3: Use prepared frosting to fill up a frosting bag with a long nozzle. Use white or yellow frosting to be more realistic.

STEP 4: Reach the frosting nozzle into the middle of the cupcakes. Push in a generous amount of frosting until you start to see frosting coming out in several places.

STEP 5: Examine the edges to see where your "vein" material appears.

STEP 6: Remove the cupcakes from the glass. If they get stuck, try again with another pair, but spray a little oil in the glass first. Once out of the glass, cut the cupcakes in half. What do you see? Think of this as a quartz vein that invaded a rock.

 Creative Enrichment

1. Try different materials, such as squeezing cheese in between two crackers.

2. Loosen up the frosting with extra milk or cream to make it runny.

THE SCIENCE BEHIND THE FUN

In this experiment, you pushed a "vein" of frosting in between layers of cake, just like a vein might force its way in between layers of rock. Your frosting took advantage of the weak bond between the layers and may have also created veins in different directions or a "reservoir" of frosting in the middle. When these are hollow in the middle, they're called *vugs*, which sometimes contain valuable gem minerals such as emeralds.

Gold miners who rushed to the Mother Lode region of California first found gold nuggets and flakes in the creeks and rivers, but they soon turned their attention to the source of all that gold. They quickly traced the gold to a large system of quartz veins that they dubbed "the Mother Lode." These veins were squeezed into place along weak cracks in the rocks, often forced in between granite intrusions and the country rocks.

Geologists believe that when intrusions force their way up into the Earth's crust and cool in place, they often leave behind a liquid that is rich in quartz and other material. We saw in earlier labs that crystals form slowly in a saturated solution, but we used simple compounds of water and salt, water and sugar, etc. The veins in mining districts are much more complex, with lots of different elements. This residual liquid can contain iron, calcium, sulfur, and precious metals. The liquids often move around when earthquakes split open the rocks and create fresh cracks. Sometimes the veins form as small coatings at first, but the hot liquid may build up under repeated pressure. Other times, the veins may flow quickly into a crack and fill it all at once. A lot happens below the Earth that we can't see, but with experiments like this one, we can make a model of how things might occur.

PRETTY PARTICLES

Use a common sparkler firework and show how streaking meteors can leave a wake of particles.

MATERIALS

- Sparklers and matches
- Small digital scale
- Lab notebook and pen or pencil
- 5'–6' (1.5–1.8 m) of white butcher paper
- Safety glasses
- Hand lens (optional)

Safety Tips

- This lab involves fire and fireworks—you need adult supervision.

- If you have long hair, tie it back and out of the way.

- Do not wear any flammable clothes, such as a windbreaker.

- Do wear safety glasses.

- Have a garden hose nearby.

- Do not touch lit end of sparkler even after extinguished.

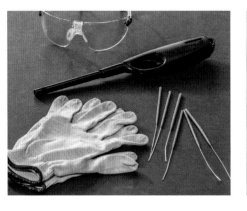

Creative Enrichment

1. What if you could capture all the smoke that your sparkler let off—what percentage of the total do you think went up as a gas?

2. Where did the rest of the mass in the unburnt sparkler end up?

PROTOCOL

STEP 1: Weigh your unburnt sparkler on the digital scale and record the weight. Some of the ends may be hanging off the scale, but you should be pretty close. If you weigh several sparklers, you'll notice there is a wide variety in their weights.

STEP 2: Spread out your butcher paper on pavement, like the sidewalk or your driveway. Don't conduct this experiment on your lawn, as you could set the grass on fire.

STEP 3: Make sure all your safety precautions are in place—safety glasses, non-loose clothing, hose near. It's best if your hose has an attachment so that all you do is squeeze the handle to get water. Turn the faucet on first if you need it on to have water flowing.

STEP 4: Light the sparkler.

STEP 5: Walk slowly along your butcher paper as the sparkler burns. Notice the blackened ash that is building up on the paper. If your sparkler lasts a long time, you may have to walk up and down several times. Make sure all the sparkles flying off are landing on your butcher paper.

STEP 6: Once the sparkler is out and cooled off, weigh it and record the weight.

STEP 7: Once the ash from the sparkler has cooled, gather it all up into a small container. You might want to look at it under a hand lens, but weigh it first and record the weight.

STEP 8: Do some math and subtract what you have left from what you started with. Calculate how small of a percentage of ash you ended up with. Convert that to a ratio, so if the unburnt sparkler was 100 percent and the wire handle was 10 percent, what percentage of material ended up as ash?

THE SCIENCE BEHIND THE FUN

This lab shows that a meteor streaking across the sky leaves telltale clues. The weight of the ash from the burning sparkler didn't add up to much—probably less than a half gram. If your original sparkler started out at 1 ounce (30 g), the math works out to a residue of only 2 percent, and probably even less.

In science, the *law of conservation of mass* says that mass can't just disappear. Since heat doesn't have any weight, the only other place that mass could be is in the smoke. More accurately, the extra mass became a gas—smoke, carbon dioxide, carbon monoxide, and other compounds.

Scientists at NASA and the University of Washington have estimated that between 5 and 300 metric tons of space rocks, meteorites, interplanetary dust, and micrometeorites reach the Earth each day. Most of that material is in the form of micrometeorites, which contain organic materials, such as amino acids, and may be part of the reason there is life on our planet.

LAB 23

MERRY METEORITES

Use marbles to watch what happens when meteorites blast out material as they impact the surface of a planet or moon.

MATERIALS

- Butcher paper, magazines, or newspapers
- Medium baking pan or plastic tub
- Flour sifter or screen
- 4 cups (500 g) of flour
- 2 cups (172 g) of cocoa powder
- 1 cup (200 g) of colored sugar
- About 3-5 marbles of different sizes, or small fishing weights, or even BBs
- Measuring tape and ruler or meter stick
- Camera (optional)

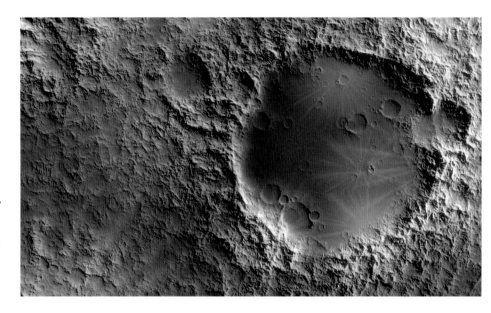

PROTOCOL

STEP 1: Spread the newspaper on the floor or on a table and place the plastic tub or pan in the center.

STEP 2: Fill the tub with sifted flour so that it is about 1 inch (2.5 cm) deep. Make it light and fluffy—don't smash it flat—and try not to have big chunks.

STEP 3: Using a sifter, sprinkle an even layer of cocoa powder over the flour. You can also swap the order of the layers to put the flour on top.

STEP 4: Sprinkle a layer of colored sugar on top. Make it nice and even.

 Safety Tips

- Avoid making a mess—you might want to do this outdoors on the lawn or driveway.

- Don't throw anything so hard that you can't control it!

STEP 5: Select your first meteorite marble.

STEP 6: Using the meter stick, select a height and drop the rock into the pan from this height. Carefully remove the rock and observe the crater it made. Measure your results.

STEP 7: Without fixing the surface, select another "meteorite" and drop it from a different height than the previous one (but drop it away from the first crater). Compare this crater with the first crater and record the difference.

STEP 8: Continue dropping the rest of your marbles from different heights so that they each make their own separate crater. Observe and compare each crater.

 Creative Enrichment

1. What happens if you use a golf ball or a tennis ball?

2. What happens if you bring your meteor in at an angle?

3. How hard is it to resist the temptation to throw something bigger or faster into the crust model?

THE SCIENCE BEHIND THE FUN

From your experiments with different heights, sizes, velocities, and angles, you should have noticed that just about every impact crater ends up being round. The *ejecta*—the material blasted out of the crater—may go in different directions but the result is usually the same.

In 1902, mining engineer D.M. Barringer learned about a large crater near Tucson, Arizona, that was known to have iron rocks around it. Today, the Barringer Meteorite Crater hosts thousands of visitors each year. While trying to prove that he had discovered an impact crater, he set up labs just like this one to test the angle of the meteor before it hit.

Every planet and moon in our solar system has occasional meteorite impacts. Most impacts are very small, but occasionally a giant meteor smashes in. Since the Earth is geologically active, with lots of erosion and earthquakes, we don't see many scars. But if you look at a full moon on a clear night, especially with binoculars or a telescope, you can clearly see some giant impact craters.

In their book *Field Guide to Meteors and Meteorites* (Springer-Verlag, 2008), O. Richard Norton and Lawrence A. Chitwood explain that the main asteroid belt lies between Mars and Jupiter, and most scientists believe those asteroids are the source of our meteors.

ROCKS OF ART

Now that you have learned more about rocks and minerals, it's time to go out and play with them. Ever since humans first started turning the things around them into tools, they have used the Earth's resources to their advantage, creating comfortable places to live by building shelters or stacking rocks to make fireplaces and walls, for example.

Rocks and minerals are also used for play and have been transformed into art objects, including using mud to make bricks and mixing materials to make paint. In these labs, you'll trace the steps that early humans took as they learned to make geology a great, creative part of their lives.

GLAMOROUS GOO

Make a batch of magnetic slime and learn a new way to play with magnetism.

MATERIALS

- 4 ounces (118 ml) white school glue
- $\frac{1}{3}$ cup (80 ml) water
- 2 tablespoons (15 g) iron oxide, ferrous oxide, or magnetic sands
- Small bowl
- Plastic spoon or spatula
- Funnel
- $\frac{1}{2}$ cup (119 ml) liquid starch
- Strong neodymium magnets

Safety Tips

- Avoid getting the slime in your eyes.

- Wash hands thoroughly after using.

- Iron oxide makes a far bigger mess than magnetic black sands. You may want to wear gloves and use plastic sheeting to prevent stains.

PROTOCOL

STEP 1: Pour the white glue into the small bowl.

STEP 2: Use a funnel to add 3 ounces (90 ml) water to the empty glue container. Swish it around in the bottle and then pour it into the bowl.

STEP 3: Add the iron oxide or magnetic black sands and stir until mixed.

STEP 4: Add the liquid starch and mix everything together. Remove the mixture from the bowl.

STEP 5: Use a strong magnet to play with the slime. You can place the magnet close to the slime and attract a long finger of material, or place a bar magnet in the slime and watch the slime cover the magnet.

Creative Enrichment

1. What other iron material can you use?

2. How well do ordinary magnets work with your slime?

THE SCIENCE BEHIND THE FUN

By combining glue, water, and liquid starch, you created an interesting goo that is fun to play with. It can stretch out to a thin sheet and it's easy to make. The science comes in because you added iron to the slime. All of the properties of magnetism are still there to play with, just in a more interesting form.

If you place a powerful magnet near the slime, you should see a small finger of magnetic material start to extend toward the magnet. If you were to freeze the slime and study a thin section under a microscope, you'd see the iron oxide lined up along the slime's magnetic field.

As planets formed while our solar system was still young, magnetism was already a powerful force. So was gravity. We still have a lot to learn about how star dust and space rocks combine into dense planets in the vacuum of space, but scientists using the Hubble Space Telescope have observed some amazing things already.

BUILDING BRICKS

Use mud, straw, and wood to make your own bricks.

MATERIALS

- **Clay-rich dirt**
- **1-quart (1 liter) wide-mouth Mason jar**
- **Water**
- **Spoon**
- **Sand (optional)**
- **Silicone ice cube trays**
- **Turkey baster**

PROTOCOL

STEP 1: For this lab, you need clay-rich soil that is sticky when wet. Mix up your sample and then let it settle, like we did in Fun with Mud (page 32). Add about 2 cups (460 g) of soil to the Mason jar. Fill the jar with water to within about an inch (2.5 cm) of the top and stir well, breaking up the chunks. Let it settle overnight. In the morning, you should have three separate bands of material: a thin layer of sand on the bottom, then silt, then clay. Ideally, you want a mixture that is about 30 percent sand and silt and 70 percent clay, but a 50-50 mix will work. Add sand or remove clay with a spoon to get the ratio right. Let it settle again.

 Safety Tips

- Messes happen any time you play around with dirt and water. It's best to do this activity outdoors!

- Be careful using the oven and use oven mitts with the hot mold.

- Ask an adult for help using the oven.

STEP 2: Select a silicone ice cube tray to use as your mold. Make sure it is clean and free of holes, dirt, etc. A pastry mold also works.

STEP 3: Use a turkey baster to remove the water from the settled jar. If you pour the water out, you will stir the mix and lose clay.

STEP 4: Stir up the mix thoroughly. Pour or spoon the clay mixture into your ice cube tray and remove any rocks or twigs.

STEP 5: Bake the mold in the oven at 150°F (65.5°C) for four hours. If there was a lot of water in the mix, remove the tray

from the oven halfway through and use a spoon to push the edges of the brick back into place. When the bricks are hard, remove from the oven and let cool. Free the bricks by flipping over the mold and tapping it lightly.

STEP 6: Dry the bricks on a paper towel. After an hour, turn them on their edges to dry some more. This whole process will take a day or two. The final moisture content of the adobe clay brick will be around 10 or 15 percent. At this point, the adobe bricks will be ready to build a tiny wall or hut.

 Creative Enrichment

1. **What happens when you vary the ratio of sand and clay?**

2. **What happens if you make your mold too thick?**

THE SCIENCE BEHIND THE FUN

Turning mud and sand into a building material is one of the great advances of civilization, dating back at least 9,000 years. Brick structures built almost 2,000 years ago still stand in India, while the Theater of Marcellus in Rome, though repaired several times, dates to 13 BCE and is the oldest Roman building to use fired bricks. In the United States, the Taos Pueblo in New Mexico, made of sun-dried mud bricks, has been continuously inhabited for more than 1,000 years.

Using rocks to make a house or fort is great if you live in a place where there are lots of rocks. But much of the land where plants grow easily is covered with sand, silt, and clay. Being able to use soil for both farming and construction is a great benefit.

Early brick makers found that if they didn't wait long enough, their bricks would quickly fall apart. One way around waiting months for bricks to dry is to fire them in an oven. You can drive the water out of the bricks and start a chemical process that binds the clay and sand together. The problem is that you need a kiln, with temperatures reaching 1,800°F (982°C), and at least a week of firing. The result is a brick that can stand up to the chemical processes that we learned about earlier.

LAB 26

MAN OF STONE

You can let your imagination run wild by using just a few flat rocks to create a mythical *inukshuk*—a stone figure to guard your garden.

MATERIALS

- Rocks
- Hammer and chisel
- Glue or superglue (optional)
- Wooden stand (optional)

Safety Tips

- Watch your fingers! It's easy to get pinched when working with heavier rocks.

- If you use a hammer to shape your rocks, use eye protection.

PROTOCOL

STEP 1: Plan your shape so that you have an idea of what rocks to collect.

STEP 2: Gather your rocks from nearby sources. You can look in streambeds, along roads in ditches, travel to ocean beaches, or go to a nearby landscape supply company. Some parks have restrictions against removing material, so learn their regulations.

STEP 3: Stack your materials and create your shape. You may find that the pieces come together perfectly, or you may want to use a hammer, chisel, or even a steel file to get the shapes exactly as you want them.

 Creative Enrichment

1. Try different materials; do you like yours rough or polished?

2. What's the fewest number of rocks you can use? What's the biggest number of rocks you can use?

3. What are the best rocks to use—basalt, schist, granite, or sandstone?

THE SCIENCE BEHIND THE FUN

An inukshuk is a "likeness of a person" in the Inuit language. The Inuit live in the far north, in the Arctic regions of Alaska, Canada, and Greenland. The Inuit built their stone figures to show that someone was once at a place, that hunting or fishing would be good here, or to tell a traveler they were on the right path. In some cases, the inukshuk was made to say someone had great power or a place was to be respected. It was considered a bad thing to destroy such symbols.

When built to help for travel, the arms of the inukshuk would point in the right direction. When created for art, the shape could vary from small and simple to quite large, with several people involved in lifting the stones. Sometimes, the Inuit would build many structures in long lines along a favorite caribou trail. They could then steer the caribou toward a waiting group of hunters.

By using stone, the inukshuk can last a long time. You can build a large one for outside in the garden, or you can create a smaller structure for your bookcase. You may need glue to make sure your inside structure doesn't fall apart and cause damage to your furniture, but keep in mind that the true power of the piece comes from its ability to stand on its own. An inukshuk symbolizes the perseverance of the Inuit people to thrive in harsh conditions.

RESOURCES

Earth Science Week classroom activities

www.earthsciweek.org/classroom-activities

Check here for many more Earth science labs you can do at home.

Identifying rocks online

www.classzone.com, select "Science" as a subject and then click on the "Earth Science" book.

This site helps you identify rocks and minerals based on streak, color, density, and other details.

ACKNOWLEDGMENTS

I'd like to thank photographer Patrick F. Smith for his patience in turning his photography studio into a science laboratory for two months, while we fine-tuned the labs and brought them to life.

ABOUT THE AUTHOR

Garret Romaine has been an avid rock hound, fossil hunter, and gold prospector for 35 years. He is a long-time journalist, columnist, and technical writer who teaches technical writing at Portland State University. He is a Fellow in the Society for Technical Communication, an organization dedicated to explaining complex technology and science. He holds a degree in geology from the University of Oregon and a degree in geography from the University of Washington. He is the author of many books on geology and the outdoors, including *The Modern Rockhounding and Prospecting Handbook, Rockhounding Idaho, Gem Trails of Oregon, Gem Trails of Washington*, and *Gold Panning the Pacific Northwest*. He is the executive director of the Rice Northwest Museum of Rocks and Minerals and also serves on the board of directors for the North American Research Group, devoted to amateur paleontologists.

INDEX